The ABC's

of

William

Penn

by: Claudie Brock

The ABC's of William Penn

by Claudie J. Brock
Illustrated by Paul Pruitt
S2 Press Edition

ISBN: 978-0-9770928-6-4
Printed by IngramSpark

First Edition

ABC book template is by "SunnyDays" - see: http://www.teacherspayteachers.com/Product/FREE-Alphabet-Book-Template-124772

Images in this book have been selected through Google Image Search with the Search Tools option chosen. Options were further set to filter in only images "labeled for reuse." The presumption is these images can be reused for this commerical project.

To
Lynmar Brock and our grandchildren

Introduction

William Penn, the Great Statesman, Philosopher, and Founder of Pennsylvania was born on October 14, 1644 (according to the old calendar) in London, England near the Tower of London.

He was educated at Oxford University in Greek, Latin, French, and German and of course English.

After listening to George Fox, the founder of The Society of Friends, or Quakers, he became convinced that this style of worship was meaningful to him, so he joined the Society of Friends himself. The Quakers were often persecuted in England, and when King Charles II wanted to repay the debt he owed to William Penn's father, he paid the debt in 1681, by granting William Penn the land across the ocean in the English colonies which became: "The Commonwealth of Pennsylvania."

William Penn agreed to accept the land for his father and decided that it would be a place where the Quakers could worship freely without interference. He planned his "Holy Experiment" in the New World, where others also could come and live in peace and harmony, and not be afraid being persecuted for his or her religion. An excellent swimmer, rower and lover of outdoor sports, William's skills and interest were ideal for the hardship of living in the new world.

Penn founded "Philadelphia," the "City of Brotherly Love" in 1682. As sole proprietor, became known for his kindness, and fair treatment of Native American Indians. He put in place for Pennsylvania a government with democratic principles, which helped inspire our United States Constitution. Ahead of his time, he proposed in an essay a plan for the "United States of Europe." This became the foundation and encouragement for the establishment of the United Nations. United Nations Day is celebrated on Penn's birthday October 14th.

William Penn wanted to call his new colony "Sylvania," but the King of England insisted that he called it "Pennsylvania" to honor his father, Admiral Sir William Penn. When the city of Philadelphia built a new City Hall, they put a monumental statue of William Penn on the tower overlooking his city of Philadelphia. Another statue can be seen at Pennsbury Manor, where Penn lived a part of the time when he was in the New World

A third statue of Penn can be seen in New Castle, Delaware, where he first landed when he came to the New World. It was sculpted by the famous Charles Parks and represents Penn receiving the key to the city, a little bit of earth, a twig and a porringer with water (a porringer is a shallow bowl). These symbols are part of the ancient English ritual that was performed when turning over a property from one person to a new owner.

Upon William Penn's death in 1718, Hannah Callowhill, Penn's second wife, was willed the full control of Penn's fortune and the Pennsylvania colony, which she administered until her death in 1727. In 1984 President Ronald Reagan made William and Hannah Penn honorary US citizens.

William Penn left a splendid legacy to the United Sates of America!

Fig. 1 - *Admiral William Penn. William Penn's father.*

A Is for Admiral William Penn, mostly known as the father of the great William Penn, founder of Pennsylvania.

Fig. 2 - *The Liberty Bell.*

B Stands for bell, the Liberty Bell, the symbol for liberty, cast for the 50th anniversary of William Penn's Charter of Privileges of 1701.

Fig. 3 - *William Penn's 1701 Charter of Privileges.*

Is for the "Charter of Privileges," the document given by William Penn to his new colony in 1701, which describes a way for a democratic type of government.

Fig. 4 - *Duels were likely fought with swords in the 17th century.*

D Is for the duel in which William Penn was involved in France for not removing his hat in front of a nobleman or doing the "the hat Honor."

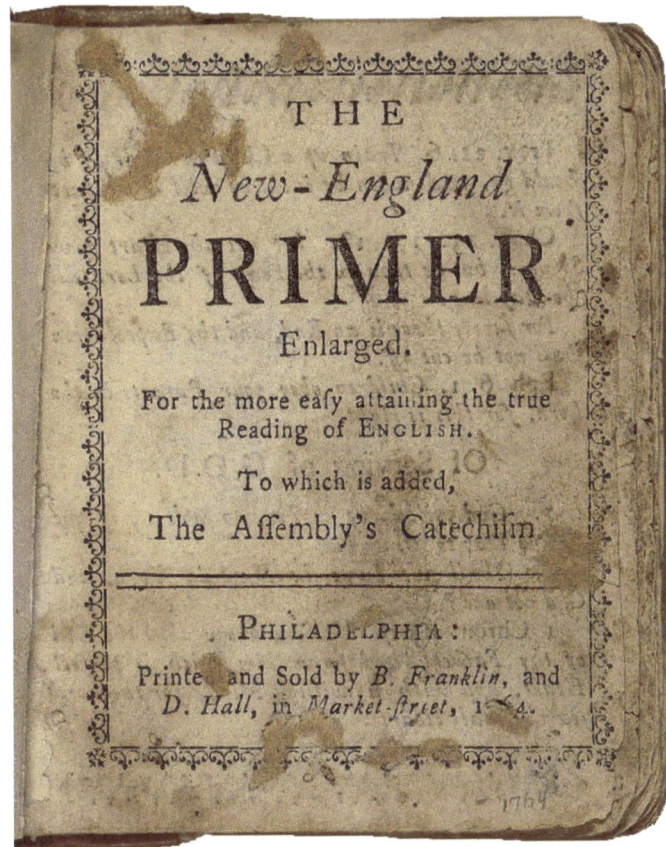

Fig. 5 - The front page from the New England Primer, an early schooltextbook in the colonies.

E Is for William Penn's education. It was very thorough and very important in Penn's life. He was very well educated, and promoted education for children. He spoke English, French, Latin, and was well versed in the legal system.

Fig. 6 - *A first draft of Penn's Frame of Government.*

Is for "Frame of Government," a contract between the proprietor William Penn and his colony of Pennsylvania.

G

Is for "Green Country Town," the name William Penn gave his new city, Philadelphia, a place where one would live near parks and enjoy nature.

Fig. 8 - *Famous painting, The Peaceable Kingdom by Elias Hicks. It's a metaphor or allegory of the Holy Experiment*

H Is for "Holy Experiment," which stands for William Penn's creation of a place where people would live together with kindness and harmony in the New World.

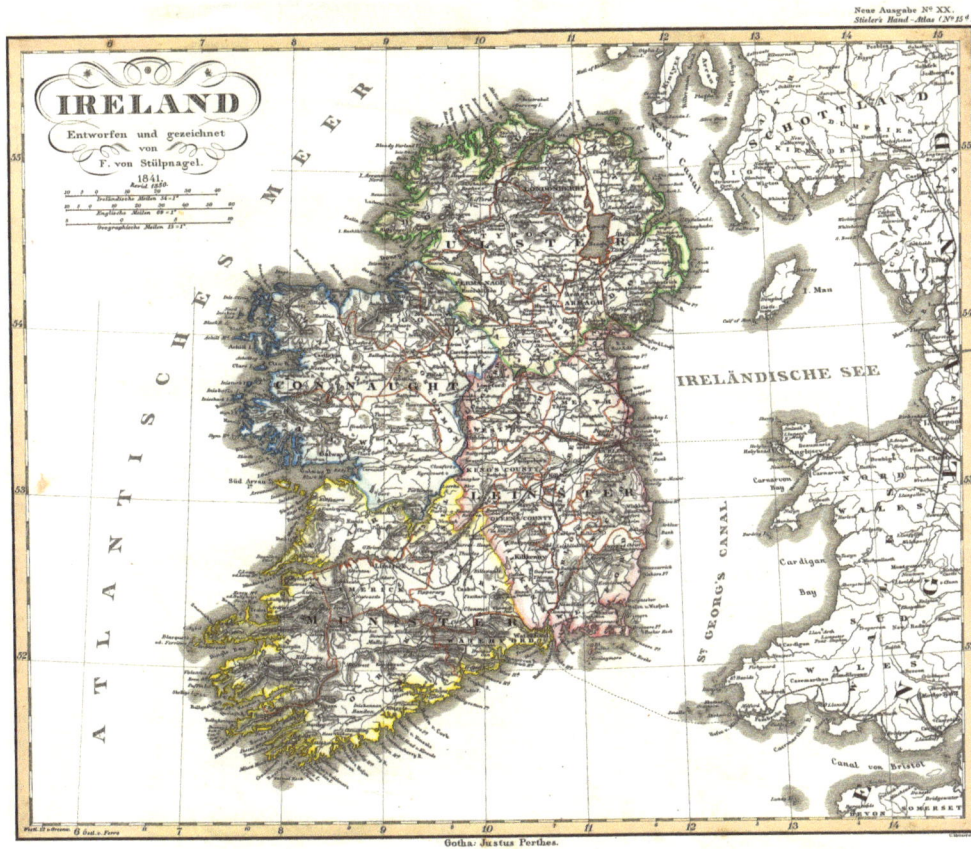

Fig. 9 - *Old map of Ireland.*

Stands for Ireland, the country next door to England, where William Penn's family had an estate. Ireland played an important role in his childhood, and later in life.

Fig. 10 - *James, Duke of York and Lord High Admiral of the English Fleet*

J

Stands for James, Duke of York and Lord High Admiral of the English fleet. He was brother to the King and very good friend of William Penn. He would help him later.

Fig. 11 - *Charles II of England in Coronation robes by John Michael Wright.*

K

Is for King Charles II, also a very good friend of William Penn's father. William's father gave King Charles II money, which helped him to get his throne back.

Fig. 12 - *A painting sybolizing a Livery of Seisin.*

L

Is for the "Livery of Seisin," a ceremony for transfering property. When William Penn came to New Castle, Delaware, which was part of his new colony, they performed the Livery of Seisin. He was given the key to the city, a bit of soil representing the land, a twig signifying the trees and some water representing the rivers.

Fig. 13 - *Sir John Vaughan, the judge in the trial.*

Is for the Mead trial, which took place in 1670. William Mead and William Penn were arrested for practicing Quakerism. The judge wanted to put their jury in jail unless they found Mead and Penn guilty. Penn knew his rights and told the judge that he could not force the jury to find them guilty. William and his friend Mead were released.

Fig. 14 - *The courthouse in New Castle Delaware.*

N Is for New Castle, the port city in Delaware where William Penn first landed when he came to the New World. New Castle was part of Penn's Three Lower Counties given to him to have access to the Delaware River.

Fig. 15 - *Goose quills were most commonly used for everyday writing. Swan quills were used when bigger letters were needed.*

O Stands for Brother "Onas," the name given to Penn by the Native Americans. Onas means in their language "a quill" made from a feather. The American Indians like to watch Penn write with a feather and ink.

15

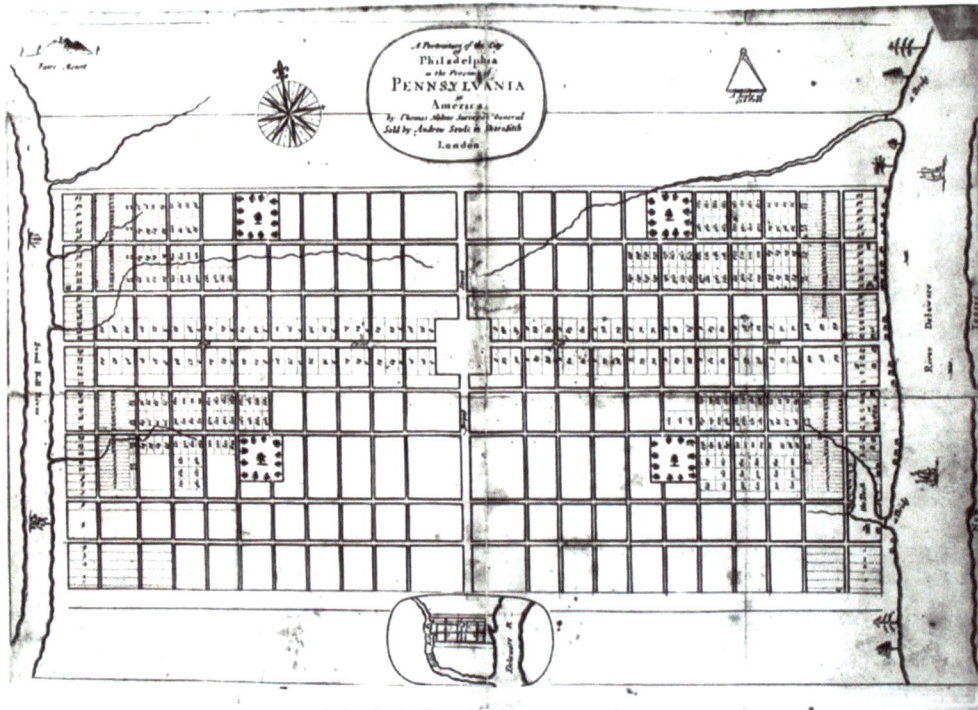

Fig. 16 - *Early planning map of Philadelphia from 1683.*

Is for Penn's Philadelphia, which means in Greek: "the City of Brotherly Love." His surveyor, Thomas Homes designed the city on Penn's land. It was originally one mile wide and two miles long and running from river to river, with five parks named: Center, Washington, Franklin, Logan, and Rittenhouse.

Fig. 17 - *This is an engraving of William Penn with a famous "Quaker type" hat.*

Q is is for Quaker. William Penn was a Quaker, and one of the most well known. He believed in non-violence and brotherly love. Unfortunately Penn was not allowed to be a Quaker in his own country.

Fig. 18 - *King Charles II granting William Penn the land of Pennsylvania, in 1681, in order for Penn to try his democratic experiment.*

R Is for rebel, William Penn was a rebel in his youth and his whole life.

Fig. 19 - *Depiction of the Shackamaxon Peace Treaty with the Indians at what would later be called the "Treaty Elm" on the Delaware River.*

S

Stands for the famous Shackamaxon Peace Treaty that took place between William Penn and the Native Americans. William Penn wanted to be friends with them and told them that he would never fight against them.

Fig. 20 - *The Tower of London.*

T Is for the Tower of London, where William Penn was a prisoner for nine months for having written an article on the Trinity. The church was angry with him because he published it without a license from the Anglican clergy.

20

Fig. 21 - *The United Nations buildings.*

Is for United Nations Day which is celebrated on William Penn's birthday, October 24th. It honors William Penn because he developed a forward-looking project for a United States of Europe, in an essay called "United Nations of Europe."

21

A good End cannot sanctify evil Means; nor must we ever do Evil, that Good may come of it. Some Folks think they may Scold, Rail, Hate, Rob and Kill too; so it be but for God's sake. But nothing in us unlike him, can please him.

- William Penn, Fruits of Solitude (1693)

Fig. 22 - *Some spiritual philosophical thoughts of William Penn.*

Stands for Victory, which William Penn deserved after his life of sufferings, and persecution for his religion. He was finally given land in the New World, where he and his friends would be free to practice their religion.

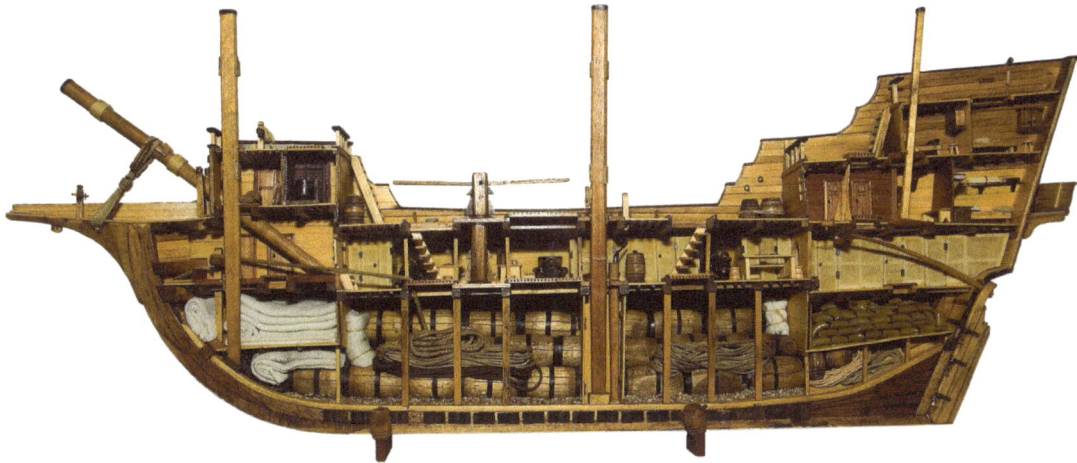

Fig. 23 - *Cut away of the Canterbury Merchant, a ship William Penn traveled to Philadelphia on in 1699. It is similar to the Welcome Ship.*

W Is for the good ship Welcome, which brought William Penn with about 100 other passengers to the New World, in order to establish his Holy Experiment.

Fig. 24 - *The William Penn statue atop city hall.*

X

Marks the cross roads of the two main streets in Philadelphia, Broad Street and Market Street. This is where City Hall stands today. On the top of this building is an enormous statute of William Penn, done by the famous sculptor Alexander Milne Calder.

24

In marriage do thou be wise: prefer the person before money, virtue before beauty, the mind before the body; then thou hast a wife, a friend, a companion, a second self.

Fig. 25 - *William Penn advice regarding marriage.*

Y

Is for "you," a word William Penn would not have used in addressing a person. The word you was too formal for Quakers. Instead he used "thee" and "thou."

Fig. 26 - *A zinnia flower*

Z Stands for Zinnia, a beautiful flower that William Penn would have enjoyed in his English garden. He loved flowers and trees, and named many streets in Philadelphia with the names of trees.

Table of Figures and Photo Credts

Fig. 1. Painting: Admiral Sir William Penn by Peter Lely - https://en.wikipedia.org/wiki/File:Lely,_William_Penn.jpg.

Fig. 2. Photo: "Liberty Bell in HDR in Philly" by Chris Favero - https://www.flickr.com/photos/cfavero/8034474794/.

Fig. 3. Document: William Penn's 1701 Chater of Privleges - http://www.amphilsoc.org/library/lobbyexhibit/shaping_north_america/case1.

Fig. 4. Wood Engraving: "The Code of Honor—A Duel In The Bois De Boulogne, Near Paris", by Godefroy Durand (Harper's Weekly, January 1875) - https://en.wikipedia.org/wiki/File:FrzDuellImBoisDeBoulogneDurand1874.jpg.

Fig. 5. Photo: The title page of the 1764 New England Primer - https://en.wikipedia.org/wiki/File:New-England_Primer_Enlarged_printed_and_sold_by_Benjamin_Franklin.jpg. Source Beinecke Rare Book & Manuscript Library, Yale University.

Fig. 6. Document: The first draft of William Penn's Frame of Government - http://bit.ly/1Cj06qB.

Fig. 7. Painting: View from Wissahickon Creek by James Peale - https://commons.wikimedia.org/wiki/File:View_on_the_wissahickon_james_peale.jpg.

Fig. 8. Painting: The Peaceable Kingdom by Edward Hicks - https://commons.wikimedia.org/wiki/File:Edward_Hicks_-_Peaceable_Kingdom.jpg.

Fig. 9. Document: Justus Perthes' Map of Ireland's Four Districts from 1841 - https://commons.wikimedia.org/wiki/File:1841_Perthes_Map_of_Ireland_-_Geographicus_-_Ireland-perthes-1841.jpg.

Fig. 10. Painting: James, Duke of York, later King James the II dressed in Romanesque costume. Portrait by Henri Gascar - https://commons.wikimedia.org/wiki/File:James,_Duke_of_York_-_Romanesque.jpg.

Fig. 11. Painting: Charles II in Coronation robes by John Michael Wright - http://www.royalcollection.org.uk/collection/404951/charles-ii-1630-1685. Royal Collection Trust / © Her Majesty Queen Elizabeth II 2015.

Fig. 12. – Painting: WPA funded mural at the Kuss Middle School in Fall River Massachusetts by John Mann ca. 1936, depicting a livery of seisin ceremony that took place in Freetown, Massachusetts in 1659 - http://www.sailsinc.org/durfee/cdpictures/mann10.jpg.

Fig. 13. – Painting: Portrait of Judge John Vaughan (1603-1674) by follower of John Michael Wright - https://commons.wikimedia.org/wiki/File:John_Vaughan_(1603-1674),_follower_of_John_Michael_Wright.jpg.

Fig. 14. – Photo: Court House, New Castle, Delaware by Pknelson - https://commons.wikimedia.org/wiki/File:Court_House,_New_Castle,_Delaware.JPG.

Fig. 15. – Photo: "Out of ink" by Jonathunder - https://commons.wikimedia.org/wiki/File:Out_of_ink.jpg.

Fig. 16. – Document: Early map of Philadelphia - https://commons.wikimedia.org/wiki/File:A_Portraiture_of_the_City_of_Philadelphia.JPG.

Fig. 17. – Engraving: William Penn, possibly by Grainger - https://en.wikipedia.org/wiki/File:William_Penn.png.

Fig. 18. - Painting: The Birth of Pennsylvania 1680 by Jean Leon Gerome Ferris - https://en.wikipedia.org/wiki/File:The_Birth_of_Pennsylvania_1680_cph.3g07157.jpg.

Fig. 19. - Painting: Penn's Treaty with the Indians at Shackamaxon by Benjamin West - https://en.wikipedia.org/wiki/File:Treaty_of_Penn_with_Indians_by_Benjamin_West.jpg.

Fig. 20. – Photo: "Tower of London viewed from the River Thames" by Bob Collowân - http://commons.wikimedia.org/wiki/File:Tower_of_London_viewed_from_the_River_Thames.jpg.

Fig. 21. - Photo: "United Nations headquarters in New York, seen from the East River" by WorldIslandInfo.com - http://commons.wikimedia.org/wiki/File:UN_HQ_157652121_5b5979da9e2.jpg.

Fig. 22. – Graphic: Quote from William Penn as found here - http://www.thefederalistpapers.org/posters/william-penn-a-good-end-cannot-sanctify-evil-means - graphic by Paul Pruitt from the William Penn stained glass image by Frederick Stymetz Lamb. Stained glass image is here: http://bit.ly/1B5jbIQ.

Fig. 23. – Photo: "Model of a 17th century English merchantman ship of about 400 tons" by Musphot This is a Canterbury Merchant Ship similar to the Welcome ship that Penn arrived on - http://commons.wikimedia.org/wiki/File:17th-century-merchantman.jpg.

Fig. 24. – Photo: "Taken in Philadelphia, Pennsylvania, in April 2006. Statue of Wikipedia:William Penn atop Philadelphia City Hall" by by Jeffrey M. Vinocur - this is a cropped version of the photo that removes the scaffolding depicted on the lower part of the image - http://en.wikipedia.org/wiki/File:Philadelphia_City_Hall-zoom.JPG.

Fig. 25. – Graphic: "You" by Paul Pruitt - William Penn quote found at http://www.brainyquote.com/quotes/quotes/w/williampen403191.html.

Fig. 26. - Photo: "This zinnia is from a flower bed on the Kungsportavenyn in Gothenberg, Sweden." by Stacey Secatch - http://commons.wikimedia.org/wiki/File:Zinnia_avenyn.jpg.

Note: The official position taken by the Wikimedia Foundation is that "faithful reproductions of two-dimensional public domain works of art are public domain."

www.ingramcontent.com/pod-product-compliance
Lightning Source LLC
Chambersburg PA
CBHW042020090426

42811CB00015B/1691